my first picture book of numbers

Written by Brian Miles
Illustrated by Anne and Ken McKie

Text © Brian Miles, 1985
Illustrations © Grandreams Ltd., 1985

© 1986 Modern Publishing, a division of Unisystems, Inc.,

PUBLISHED BY MODERN PUBLISHING
A Division of Unisystems, Inc.
New York, New York 10022

Printed in Singapore

1~one

1 raisin loaf

1 2 3 4 5 6 7 8 9 10

2~two

2 red shoes

1 **2** 3 4 5 6 7 8 9 10

3~three

3 birds in a tree

1 2 3 4 5 6 7 8 9 10

4 ~ four

4 windows in the door

1 2 3 **4** 5 6 7 8 9 10

5~five

5 bees around the hive

1 2 3 4 5 6 7 8 9 10

6~six

6 fluffy chicks

1 2 3 4 5 **6** 7 8 9 10

7~seven

7 days in a week

MONDAY 1
TUESDAY 2
WEDNESDAY 3
THURSDAY 4
FRIDAY 5
SATURDAY 6
SUNDAY 7

1 2 3 4 5 6 **7** 8 9 10

8~eight

8 bars in the gate

1 2 3 4 5 6 7 8 9 10

9~nine

9 trees in a line

1 2 3 4 5 6 7 8 9 10

10~ten

10 chicks and a hen

1 2 3 4 5 6 7 8 9 10

11~eleven

11 musical instruments

11 12 13 14 15 16 17 18 19 20

12~twelve

12 months in a year

January

February

March

April

May

June

July

August

September

October

November

December

11 **12** 13 14 15 16 17 18 19 20

13~thirteen

13 ducks on the pond

11 12 13 14 15 16 17 18 19 20

14~fourteen

14 children standing
on line

11 12 13 **14** 15 16 17 18 19 20

15~fifteen

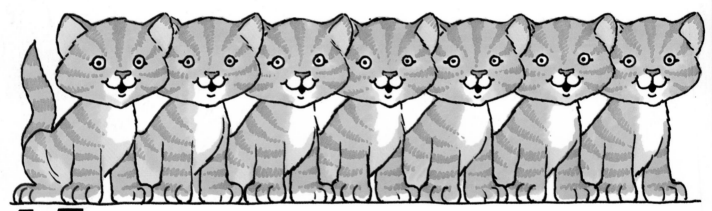

15 cats that
look alike

16~sixteen

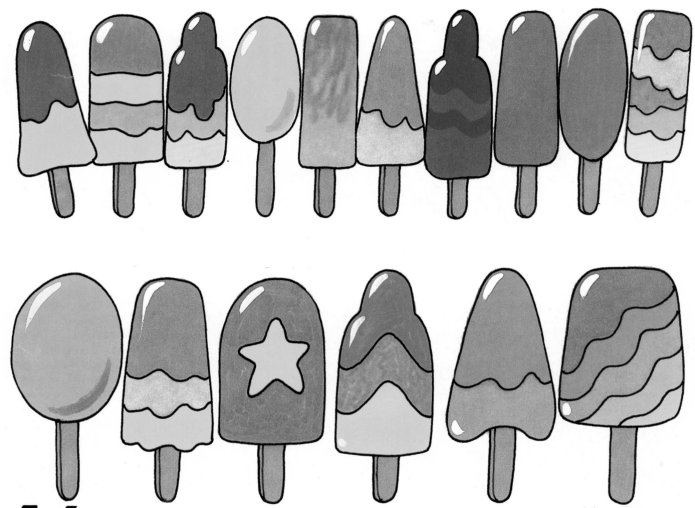

16 ice pops of many different flavors

11 12 13 14 15 16 17 18 19 20

17~seventeen

17 flowers growing tall

18~eighteen

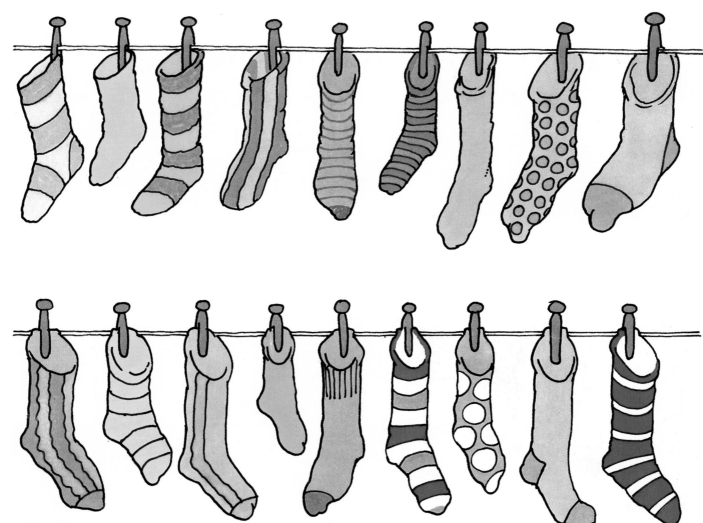

18 socks hanging
on the line

11 12 13 14 15 16 17 18 19 20

19~nineteen

19 pencils for coloring fun

11 12 13 14 15 16 17 18 **19** 20

20~twenty

20 bottles of different shapes and sizes

30~thirty

30 candles on the cake

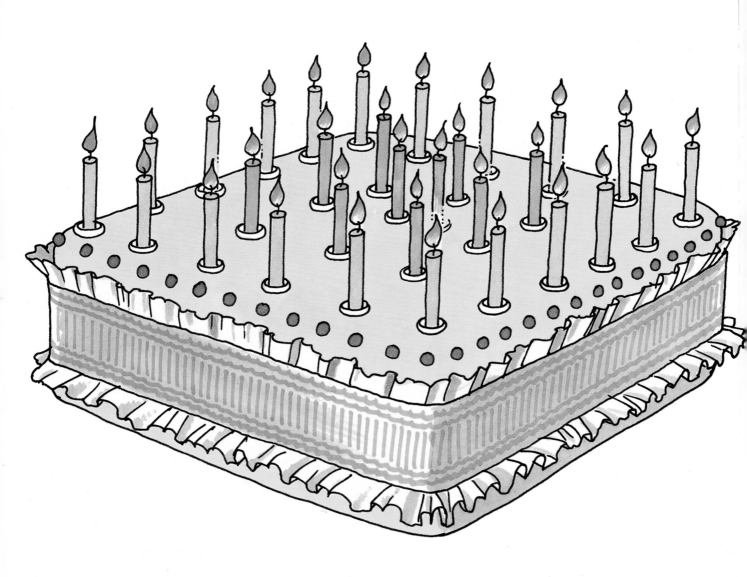

10 20 **30** **40** 50

40~forty

40 apples ready for picking

60 70 80 90 100

50~fifty

50 rocks in the river

10   20   30   40   **50**

60~sixty

60 minutes on the clock

60 70 80 90 100

70~seventy

70 pieces of fruit
ten of each in a row

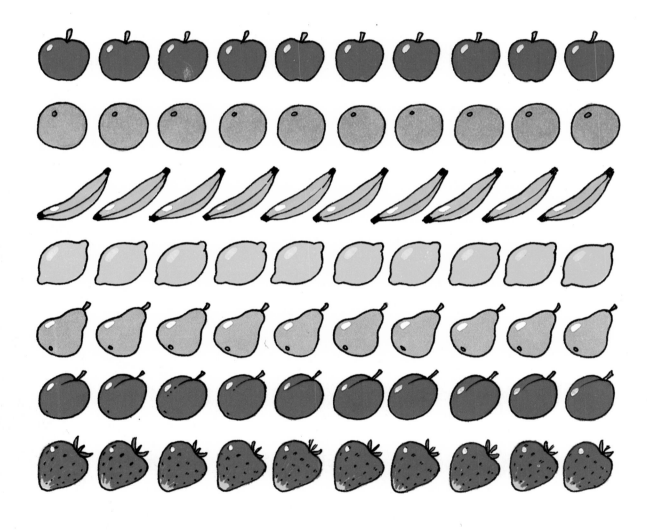

10   20   30   40   50

80~eighty

80 objects
ten of each placed
side by side

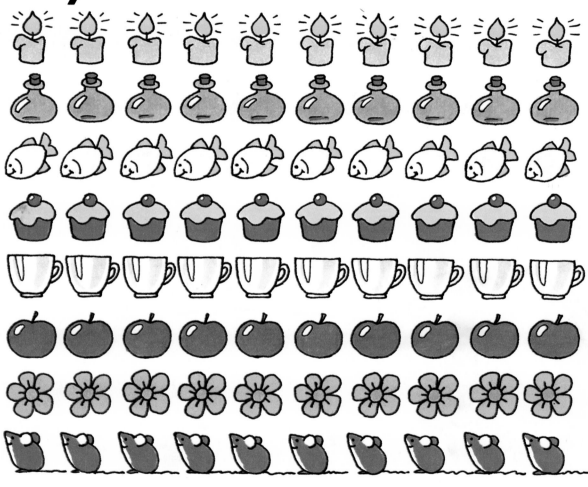

| 60 | 70 | 80 | 90 | 100 |

90~ninety

90 objects for you to count

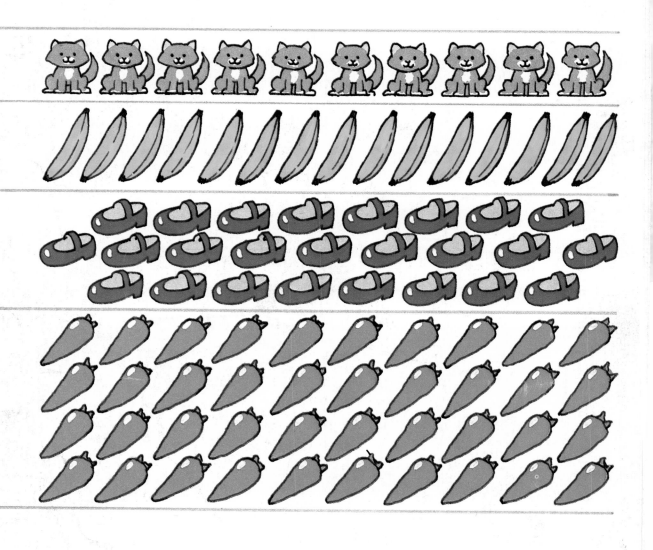

10 20 30 40 50